HOW TO CATALOGUE

By the same author:

Buying books for libraries ISBN 0-85157-428-9

HOW TO CATALOGUE

a practical handbook using
AACR2 and Library of Congress

Second edition

Liz Chapman
Librarian
Institute of Economics and Statistics
University of Oxford

CLIVE BINGLEY LONDON

© Liz Chapman 1984, 1990

Published by
Library Association Publishing Ltd
7 Ridgmount Street
London WC1E 7AE

First edition published 1984
This second edition published 1990

British Library Cataloguing in Publication Data

Chapman, Liz
  How to catalogue: a practical handbook using AACR2 and
  Library of Congress − 2nd ed.
  1. Documents. Cataloguing. Machine-readable files: LC
  MARC records. Use by library cataloguing departments
  I. Title
  025.3′028′557

  ISBN 0-85157-427-0

Typeset in 10/12pt Palacio and 10/12pt Univers by Library Association Publishing Ltd
Printed and made in Great Britain by Redwood Press Ltd, Trowbridge, Wilts.

CONTENTS

INTRODUCTION TO THE SECOND EDITION

During the last decade, the way in which cataloguing work in libraries is organized has changed considerably. Many libraries now have access to automation. This is probably particularly the case in libraries which use Library of Congress classification and Subject Headings. Library of Congress has adapted reasonably well to automation compared with some other schemes, and indeed some libraries when automating their procedures have switched to LC and/or LCSH.

As a result of the publication of the consolidated 1988 version of AACR2, a new edition of this handbook was suggested by the publisher. This second edition has been substantially revised from the first to reflect not only AACR2 changes but also changes in LC practice, particularly in the area of subject headings.

Meanwhile, the author has moved away from Brunel University Library. As a result, the handbook too has moved away from Brunel practice to provide a more general picture. This implies no disrespect to Brunel where the handbook was originally hatched and the author learned practical cataloguing.

This handbook is based on the 'mark and park' principle of cataloguing: take your cataloguing records from a centralized source as far as possible and follow standard editing procedures. However, the book does not concentrate specifically on automation since there are still many LC libraries in the world which will not have access to automation for some time to come. At any rate this is not the place to describe all the possibilities. MARC systems differ from country to country and, since the first edition of this handbook was well received outside the UK, it was decided not to go into the complexities of MARC.

The handbook is therefore intended to help in the process of creating consistent catalogue records in any format. It is intended for libraries with a minimum of professional staff time available for cataloguing and where library assistants are involved in creating catalogue records. It should also be useful to library students. It covers the standard procedures in cataloguing using AACR2 (1988 revision) and Library of Congress data from centralized sources.

Cataloguers should refrain from meddling with LC data – it will only make their jobs more difficult later on. The handbook should be used in order to create catalogues which help users to find what they want in the library.

ACKNOWLEDGEMENTS
The acknowledgements in the first edition still stand and I am grateful to those organizations who kindly gave me information and further permission for the reproduction of copyright material: the British Library, the Library of Congress and the Library Association.

I would also like to thank all those people whose continued help and encouragement meant that I was able to get this second edition finished, including David Thomas and Nick Childs at Brunel University Library and Charles Ellis and Barbara Jover at Library Association Publishing. I am also grateful to those reviewers of the first edition who made constructive comments and criticisms.

1989 is proving to be a year of considerable personal and professional ups and downs and I would like to thank those people who have given me the necessary support and encouragement to continue writing. Special mention should be made of the staff of the Library of the Institute of Economics and Statistics, of Gwen Hampshire and of Jackie and Steve Woolgar. My family, however, bore the brunt of the work, trying hard to keep quiet while I 'wasted' the weekends. Frankie and Isabelle deserve more of my time but Frank taught me how to work hard.

Oxford
1 July 1989

ABBREVIATIONS

These abbreviations either occur in this handbook or are likely to occur in cataloguing with LC and AACR2. There is a more extensive list in Appendix B of AACR2.

AACR2	Anglo-American cataloguing rules (2nd edition)
ALA	American Library Association
A/V	Audio-visual
BBIP	British Books in Print
BIE	Books in English
BIP	Books in Print (USA)
BL	British Library
BLBSD	British Library Bibliographic Services Division
BNB	British National Bibliography
c	copyright (date)
ca	circa
CD – ROM	Compact Disc – Read only memory
CIP	Cataloguing in Publication
CLA	Canadian Library Association
col.	colour
COM	Computer Output Microform
COMARC	COoperative MAchine Readable Cataloguing
comp.	compiler
DC	Dewey (Decimal) classification
e.g.	for example
ed.	editor/edition
EMMA	Extra-MARC MAterial
et al.	and others
IFLA	International Federation of Library Associations
ill.	illustrations/illustrator
ISBN	International Standard Book Number
ISSN	International Standard Serial Number
J	Journal
LA	Library Association (UK)
LC	Library of Congress
LCSH	Library of Congress Subject Headings
MARC	MAchine Readable Cataloguing

min.	minutes
mm.	millimetres
NLM	National Library of Medicine (USA) (sometimes DNLM, D standing for DC as in Washington DC)
no.	number
NUC	National Union Catalog
p.	page(s)
pbk.	paperback
rev.	revised
SAE	Series added entry
sd.	sound
S.l.	no place (of publication)
s.n.	no name (of publisher)
tr.	translator
UDC	Universal Decimal Classification
v./vol.	volume(s)

ARRANGEMENT OF THE HANDBOOK

The handbook follows the arrangement of the first edition – alphabetical by topic. Cross-referencing is facilitated by the use of capital letters to indicate another relevant section. Square brackets [ ] imply a procedure which can be regarded as optional.

The major relevant AACR2 rule numbers are quoted in brackets at the head of each topic.

There is a brief bibliography which also includes other books which will be helpful in cataloguing with AACR2 and Library of Congress.

ADDED COPIES (and reprints by the same publisher)

(a) Check existing record in the CATALOGUE. Verify LC CLASS NUMBER making sure the added copy is the same edition. NEW EDITIONS have separate instructions.
(b) Correct number of copies in catalogue.
(c) Write LC CLASS NUMBER on verso title page with copy number, e.g. cop. 3.
(d) Send item for PROCESSING with relevant information.

Below is an example of an entry where the library has three copies. On catalogue cards it is best to make alterations in pencil to ease later correction.

Taylor, Lance

Macro models for developing countries. – London : McGraw-Hill, 1979.
   271p. – (Economics handbooks series)

Includes bibliographies.
ISBN 0 – 07 – 063135 – 2

3 copies

HC59.7.T39

ADDED ENTRIES (21.29, 21.30)

Added entries are also known as tracings or access points in the catalogue.

Added entries for SUBJECT HEADINGS are indicated by Arabic numerals 1, 2, 3, 4. . . .

They give the subject matter of the item by LC SUBJECT HEADINGS.

Added entries for authors, titles, series, sponsor etc. are indicated by Roman numerals I, II, III, IV. . . . In an online catalogue these are generated automatically from the description.

They provide further points of access for library users who may not have a complete reference to check.

Added entries are found at the bottom of the catalogue entry. They can be typed across the top of the entry or highlighted in tracings in manual catalogues.

Taylor, Lance

Macro models for developing countries. –
London : McGraw – Hill, 1979.
271p. – (Economics handbooks series)

Includes bibliographies.
ISBN 0 – 07 – 063135 – 2

1. Developing countries   2. Economic development –
Mathematical models   3. Macroeconomics –
Mathematical models I. Title II. Series

HC59.7.T39

In this example the added entries for SUBJECT HEADINGS are:
- Developing countries
- Economic development – Mathematical models
- Macroeconomics – Mathematical models.

The other added entries are:
- Macro models for developing countries
- Economics handbooks series.

AUTHOR MAIN HEADING (21.1A2)

The MAIN HEADING in the catalogue is usually the author's name where this is given in the book, or the first named author where there are up to three authors. In other cases books are entered under the title, i.e. TITLE MAIN HEADING. For other types of MAIN HEADING *see* CONFERENCES and CORPORATE BODIES. Where a book is entered under an author's name there will be ADDED ENTRIES for the title (and up to two other authors as necessary).

Webster, Frank

Information technology : a Luddite analysis / Frank Webster and Kevin Robins. – Norwood, N.J. : Ablex, 1986.
   387p. – (Communication and information science)

Bibliography : p. 349 – 375.

ISBN 0 – 89391 – 343 – X

1. Electronic data processing 2. Information storage and retrieval systems – Sociological aspects I. Title II. Robins, Kevin

QA76.W33

In this example the MAIN HEADING is the first author's name with ADDED ENTRIES for the title and second author.

[Some LC records include the date of birth after an author's name. If you need to do this to differentiate between two otherwise identical names, check NAME AUTHORITIES for the information. Otherwise date of birth can be omitted.]

AUTHORITY FILES (22.3,26.2A2)

These files are maintained by library staff in order to ensure continuity and consistency in the catalogues. They show 'approved' forms of catalogue entries.

(a) *AUTHOR/NAME AUTHORITY*
A file of accepted forms of names with a note of any references from unused forms. It prompts the making of 'see' references for the CATALOGUE. It is compiled with reference to LC NAME AUTHORITIES and AACR2.[1,2] The examples show a double-barrelled or hyphenated surname, a CORPORATE BODY and a change of name.

Name authority

```
Milne-Bailey, W

x Bailey, W    Milne-
```

prompts the making of this entry for the CATALOGUE:

```
Bailey, W    Milne-

SEE

Milne-Bailey, W
```

CORPORATE BODY name authority

```
Great Britain. Army. Royal Signals

x Royal Signals
x Great Britain. Royal Signals
```

prompts the making of these two entries for the CATALOGUE:

```
Royal Signals
SEE
Great Britain. Army. Royal Signals
```

```
Great Britain. Royal Signals
SEE
Great Britain. Army. Royal Signals
```

Some names, particularly those of CORPORATE BODIES change over time and it helps library users if the library provides explanatory references in the catalogues. These direct users to earlier and later forms of names. A record should be kept in the authority file in case further changes need to be made or the original entries withdrawn.

Examples of explanatory references

```
Great Britain. Department of Transport.
Highway Engineering Computer Branch
for earlier works published before 1976
SEE
Great Britain. Department of the Environment.
Highway Engineering Computer Branch
```

```
Great Britain. Department of the Environment.
Highway Engineering Computer Branch
for later works published after 1976
SEE
Great Britain. Department of Transport.
Highway Engineering Computer Branch
```

These entries are filed in the CATALOGUE before any entries with the heading as at the top of the explanatory reference.

(b) *SERIES AUTHORITY*

A file of SERIES held in the library which shows whether the CATALOGUE has a SERIES ADDED ENTRY (SAE) as well as any unused formats for the particular series so that 'see' references can be made. An entry should be made in the series authority file for each new series as it arises in cataloguing copy, and a decision made about whether series ADDED ENTRIES are required. In general, publishers' series are not given ADDED ENTRIES unless it is likely that library users will look for them. The examples show (a) an accepted series, (b) a rejected series and (c) a series with possible variant formats.

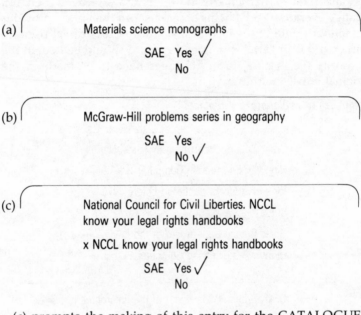

(a)
Materials science monographs
SAE Yes ✓
No

(b)
McGraw-Hill problems series in geography
SAE Yes
No ✓

(c)
National Council for Civil Liberties. NCCL know your legal rights handbooks
x NCCL know your legal rights handbooks
SAE Yes ✓
No

(c) prompts the making of this entry for the CATALOGUE:

NCCL know your legal rights handbooks

SEE

National Council for Civil Liberties. NCCL know your legal rights handbooks

(c) *SUBJECT AUTHORITY*
A file showing the SUBJECT HEADINGS used in the CATALOGUE with their relevant references. The file is used when making WITHDRAWALS since referral to it can ensure that all appropriate subject entries and references are removed. It is filed by LC FILING. LC SUBJECT HEADINGS provide for a structure of inter-relating references, which can be reflected in the library's catalogue. Instructions for setting up the references file are included under SUBJECT HEADINGS. An online catalogue can provide access to all LC SUBJECT HEADINGS to ensure consistent application.

Subject authority

> **Fighting (Psychology)**
>
> UF   Combativeness
>   Pugnacity
>
> RT   Aggressiveness (Psychology)

prompts the making of these three references for the CATALOGUE:

> Combativeness
>
> use
>
> Fighting (Psychology)

> Pugnacity
>
> use
>
> Fighting (Psychology)

> Fighting (Psychology)
>
> related term
>
> Aggressiveness (Psychology)

7

BOOKS IN ENGLISH (BIE)[3]

Books in English is a microfiche bibliography of English-language titles produced by the British Library Bibliographical Services Division. It covers only English-language titles, but these are from all over the world. It also includes data contributed by the Library of Congress (COMARC).

The service is available on microfiche from 1971. There is a single sequence cumulation available for 1971–80 and 1981–5. Annual listings are available and the current subscription provides for bi-monthly cumulated issues with a full annual cumulation. All subject areas are covered, including fiction.

The arrangement of *Books in English* follows AACR2. Full details for each book can be found only under the MAIN HEADING. So, for example, if a book is by a single author and you find it via the title (or the SERIES) you will need to check the entry under the author's name, since it is only here that you will find the full bibliographical information.

There are few cross-references in *Books in English* and you must check whether an incomplete entry implies CIP (CATALOGUING IN PUBLICATION) information or whether you have simply found an ADDED ENTRY and need to check further for the MAIN HEADING. *Books in English* often contains CIP information but it is not marked as such. A lack of information about the book will be the main indicator of CIP. *Books in English* will give you the following basic information: author, title, other authors up to a total of three, edition, place of publication, publisher, date of publication, number of pages, size, binding (if not cloth), Library of Congress SUBJECT HEADINGS (but sometimes suspect), Library of Congress class number, Dewey class number, control number, BNB number.

The control number will usually be the ISBN. (Many libraries use ISBNs as control numbers in their circulation systems.) However, when the ISBN is not available the BNB number (B..–.....) or the LC number (LC..–......) will be used instead. Numbers which begin with DC are the Dewey class numbers.

The examples show a full MAIN ENTRY and title ADDED ENTRY from *Books in English*.

Full MAIN ENTRY

WEST, Rebecca
   Black lamb and grey falcon. – Rev. ed. – London :
   Papermac, 1982, c1941. – 1181p ; 20cm pbk. – £6.95
   1. Yugoslavia – Description and travel
   DR1221 DC914.97'0421 CONTROL NO: 0-333-33492-2
   B82-35079

Title ADDED ENTRY

BLACK lamb and grey falcon : a journey through Yugoslavia /
   by Rebecca West. – London : Papermac, 1982, c1941
   DR1221 DC914.97'0421 CONTROL NO: 0-333-33492-2

CATALOGUE

An alphabetical sequence of catalogue entries relating to material held in the library. It is filed according to LC FILING RULES[4] and provides several access points for each item catalogued.

There may also be TEMPORARY CATALOGUE ENTRIES for items not yet catalogued and/or still on order.

SUBJECT ADDED ENTRIES
ADDED ENTRIES with LC SUBJECT HEADINGS for material in the library arranged in an alphabetical sequence according to LC FILING RULES. Designated by 1, 2, 3 . . . on cataloguing copy.

AUTHOR/TITLE/SERIES ADDED ENTRIES
ADDED ENTRIES for: additional authors or editors (to a total of three), title, editor, series etc. Designated by I, II, III . . . on cataloguing copy. These ADDED ENTRIES are generated automatically or can be accessed according to coding in automated catalogues.

SHELFLIST/OFFICIAL CATALOGUE
This is the library staff's working catalogue in which can be noted official details such as 'missing 1981', 'copy 4 withdrawn 1975' etc. It is not normally available to library users. In an online catalogue, passwords control access to different parts of the catalogue.

CATALOGUE ENTRIES – **Examples** (Chapter 1)

Author main heading

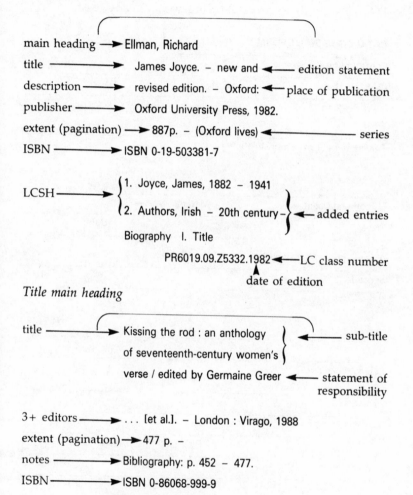

main heading → Ellman, Richard

title → James Joyce. – new and ← edition statement

description → revised edition. – Oxford: ← place of publication

publisher → Oxford University Press, 1982.

extent (pagination) → 887p. – (Oxford lives) ← series

ISBN → ISBN 0-19-503381-7

LCSH →
1. Joyce, James, 1882 – 1941
2. Authors, Irish – 20th century – ← added entries
Biography I. Title

PR6019.09.Z5332.1982 ← LC class number

date of edition

Title main heading

title → Kissing the rod : an anthology
of seventeenth-century women's ← sub-title
verse / edited by Germaine Greer ← statement of responsibility

3+ editors → ... [et al.]. – London : Virago, 1988

extent (pagination) → 477 p. –

notes → Bibliography: p. 452 – 477.

ISBN → ISBN 0-86068-999-9

LCSH →
1. English poetry – Early modern, 1500 – 1700
2. Women poets I. Greer, Germaine (ed.) ← editor added entry

PR1209.K57 ← LC class number

11

CATALOGUE INPUT FORM

This is a sample form which can be used for ORIGINAL CATA-LOGUING, where no cataloguing copy already exists.

CATALOGUE INPUT FORM

Control number						
Class number						

Main Heading

Title/statement of responsibility. —

Edition statement.—	Material type.—	
Place:	Publisher,	Date:

Extent
(Pagination or no. of vols.).—   ill.

Series (   )

Notes.—

ISBN

Subject headings
1.

2.

3.

4.

Added entries   I, II, III . . .

Title   Series

12

CATALOGUING IN PUBLICATION (CIP)

Many publishers now provide pre-publication information on books to the British Library and Library of Congress for cataloguing purposes. The MARC contributors then catalogue and classify the book and provide SUBJECT HEADINGS as far as they are able. This information is printed in the book when it is published. It usually appears on the verso title page. It is incomplete since the physical description of the book, for example, is not available until publication. However, suitably edited, it can be made into an acceptable catalogue entry, and will avoid possibly delay while other cataloguing copy is sought or created. If there are two CIP entries in the book choose the one from Library of Congress, although you may have to alter the ISBN. CIP entries appear in BOOKS IN ENGLISH[3] and MARCFICHE.[5] It may be necessary, when CIP data is upgraded into a fuller record in the MARC database, to alter the library's entry if any changes are made by the cataloguing agency. More than 20 countries have their own CIP programmes, but beware: they are not all MARC compatible, using different cataloguing rules.

British Library CIP records printed in books since late 1987 do not include LC subject data but this is available to some extent for libraries which have online access to BL cataloguing records. Some publishers do not print CIP information in books although they may indicate that it is available from the cataloguing agency. This is an example of a recent CIP entry published in a book. 320'.01 is a Dewey number.

Bodanis, David

Web of words : the ideas behind politics.

1. Political science

I. Title

320'.01   JA71

ISBN 0-333-38975-1 (hardcover)

ISBN 0-333-38976-X (hardcover)

CENTRALIZED/CO-OPERATIVE CATALOGUING

Libraries which use LC for classification and SUBJECT HEADINGS are able to obtain data from a variety of sources, particularly if they have access online to one of the services offering LC data. National services such as the British Library have licensing arrangements with individual libraries for the use of their records.

MICROFICHE
Library of Congress cataloguing is available on microfiche from:
- Library of Congress (NUC)[6]
- Library Corporation (MARCFICHE)[5]
- British Library (BOOKS IN ENGLISH).[3]

ONLINE
Online access to LC data is available via:
- Bibliographic utilities such as OCLC
- Co-operative or consortium networks for libraries such as BLCMP
- National library services such as BLAISE-LINE
- Commercial online services such as DIALOG.

COMPACT DISC
The Library Corporation provides LC data on CD-ROM. This service is known as *Bibliofile* and is basically the same as MARCFICHE although it provides greater flexibility in access. Library of Congress is also developing its own CD-ROM products.

These services are particularly useful for retrospective conversion of catalogue records from manual to machine readable.

CONFERENCES (symposia, meetings, colloquia, seminars, congresses, workshops, conventions) (24.7)

According to AACR2, conferences are treated in catalogue entries as if they were CORPORATE BODIES. The definition of a corporate body is 'an organization or group of persons that is identified by a particular name and that acts, or may act, as an entity' (AACR2).[2]

If a conference has a distinctive name, the MAIN HEADING is that name. This is followed by (number : date : place) where these are given in the publication. In this way, a series of conferences can file chronologically in the catalogue. Pre-AACR2 headings found in older catalogues will need to be altered. The date of the conference, not its publication date (although these may coincide), should be added to the end of the LC CLASS NUMBER.

There will be ADDED ENTRIES for:

- SUBJECT HEADINGS
- Title – if this differs from MAIN HEADING
- Editor(s) – if named (up to a maximum of 3)
- Sponsor(s) – if named
- Series – if part of a series.

Conferences often have a large number of ADDED ENTRIES to help library users to locate the item. However, entries are not made for the authors of individual papers.

Conferences can be CONTINUATIONS of stock already held in the library but each should have an individual catalogue entry. Indeed, some which are produced regularly are treated as SERIALS for classification, but may still have individual cataloguing. A series of conferences may share an LC CLASS NUMBER but each will have its own date and may have different SUBJECT HEADINGS.

N.B. Do not alter dates found in classes D and J which are part of the LC CLASS NUMBER before the CUTTER NUMBER.

The examples show:

(a) MAIN HEADING conference title ... (no. : date : place)
(b) Date of conference at end of LC CLASS NUMBER
(c) ADDED ENTRIES:

15

- SUBJECT HEADINGS
- Series
- Editor
- Sponsors.

Rocky Mountain Bioengineering
Symposium (11th : 1974 : Colorado Springs)

Proceedings ...
R856.R63.1974

Rocky Mountain Bioengineering
Symposium (12th : 1975 : Denver)

Proceedings of the twelfth Rocky Mountain
bioengineering symposium ... April 28 – 30, 1975,
University of Colorado Denver, Colorado / edited by K.C.
Rock. –
Pittsburgh : Instrument Society of America, 1975.
    192p. : ill. – (Biomedical sciences instrumentation ;
v.11)

Sponsored by Instrument Society of America.
Biomedical Sciences Division and IEEE Group on
Engineering in Medicine and Biology.

ISBN 0 – 83664 – 263 – 6

1. Biomedical engineering – Addresses, essays, lectures
2. Biology – Addresses, essays, lectures I. Series II.
Rock, K.C. (ed.) III. Instrument Society of America.
Biomedical Sciences Division IV. Institute of Electrical and
Electronics Engineers. Group on Engineering in Medicine
and Biology
R856.R63.1974

N.B. NAME AUTHORITIES[1] can be used to verify the MAIN
HEADING for a conference.

CONTINUATIONS (2.5B17 – 22, 2.5B6)

Continuations are single volumes, supplements or parts of a recognizable multi-volume monograph work where the library already holds at least one other of the set. They may be CONFERENCES where the library already has others in the SERIES. They are dealt with as follows:

(a) Amend catalogue record for previous volume, adding information on the latest volume acquired, or create new record for each volume. If there are major differences between volumes, separate records are preferable, *see* SERIES.

(b) If separate volumes have individual titles and/or authors/editors, these should be described and given ADDED ENTRIES to help library users as the example shows. This should also ensure that the library does not buy an item it already has in stock. (For this very reason of unintentional duplication, the LC practice of SERIES CLASSIFICATION should be avoided.)

(c) Write LC CLASS NUMBER as for previous volumes on verso title page with 'vol.2, vol.3' etc. at end.

(d) Send item to PROCESSING with relevant information.

(e) N.B. The date of publication is left open until the multi-volume work is complete.

Example of catalogue entry for a continuation

Handbook of learning and cognitive processes
/ edited by W.K. Estes. – Hillsdale,
   N.J. : Erlbaum, 1975 –
   v.1 – 3

Contents:

   v.1 Introduction to concepts and issues
   v.2 Conditioning and behavior therapy
   v.3 Approaches to human learning and motivation

1. Cognition 2. Learning, Psychology of
I. Estes, W.K. (ed.) II. Title vol.1
III. Title vol.2 IV. Title vol.3

BF311.H334

CORPORATE BODIES (21.1B, 24)

Corporate bodies exist where a single name, often an acronym, identifies a group of people or an organization. Those which occur most commonly are:

- government agencies
- commercial companies
- associations
- CONFERENCES

Where the corporate body is responsible for the work being catalogued its name forms the MAIN HEADING. Conventional names should be used unless the official name is in common use. In the case of UK government publications, the conventional name is United Kingdom but many agencies continue to use the more familiar Great Britain as do LCSH and this handbook.

Great Britain. Department of Health

Health and personal social services
statistics. – Norwich: HMSO, 1989.

. . . . .

RA241.A1.H42

Lloyds Bank

Sweden: economic report. – London:
Lloyds Bank, 1986.

. . . . .

HC373.L46

Organisation for Economic Co-operation
and Development

Ageing populations: the social policy
implications. – Paris: OECD, 1988.

. . . . .

HQ1061.O73

CUTTER NUMBERS

Cutters numbers are made up of a letter followed by one or more digits. These numbers (named after Charles A. Cutter, an American librarian on whose ideas the LC classification scheme is based) are allocated to each item in the library and this allows for the shelving in order of items within a particular class. No two books in the same class should have the same cutter number. The numbers are allocated according to a specific CUTTER TABLE. The cutter number usually indicates the MAIN HEADING i.e. the author of the book or its title. However, double cutter numbers occur where the classification number is broken down for greater specificity.[7] Generally, the first cutter number is then part of the subject classification (CLASS NUMBER) and the second is for the author/title. But it is possible for a second cutter to represent, for example, form, or a geographical area, and not the author's name or the book's title.[8] In this case, only the second cutter can be altered, decimally, to provide an alphabetical shelf order.

Bates, Grace Elizabeth
  Probability / by Grace E. Bates
                QA273.B385_____Author cutter

Piggott, Michael R
  Load-bearing fibre composites. – Oxford :
  Pergamon, 1980.
                TA418.9.C6P54_____Subject:
                                    composites;
                                    + author cutter

Elliott Newspaper Group
  Advertising directory. – Mildura : Elliott
  Newspaper Group, 1968-
                HF5808.A82V54_____Country: Australia;
                                    Area: Victoria; no
                                    cutter for heading

CUTTER TABLE

'Library of Congress book numbers are composed of the initial letter of the MAIN ... HEADING followed by Arabic numerals representing the succeeding letters on the following basis:

1 After initial vowels

for the 2nd letter:	b	d	l,m	n	p	r	s,t	u-y
use number:	2	3	4	5	6	7	8	9

2 After initial letter S

for the 2nd letter:	a	ch	e	h,i	m-p	t	u
use number:	2	3	4	5	6	7-8	9

3 After initial letters Qu

for the 3rd letter:	a	e	i	o	r	y
use number:	3	4	5	6	7	9
for names beginning:	Qa-Qt					
use numbers:	2-29					

4 After other initial consonants

for the 2nd letter:	a	e	i	o	r	u	y
use number:	3	4	5	6	7	8	9

5 When an additional number is preferred

for the 3rd letter:	a-d	e-h	i-l	m	n-q	r-t	u-w	x-z
use number:	2*	3	4	5	6	7	8	9

(optional for 3rd letter a or b.)

'Letters not included in these tables are assigned the next higher or lower number as required by previous assignments in the particular class.'

CUTTER NUMBER EXAMPLES

'The arrangements in the following examples illustrate some possible applications of these tables:

1 Names beginning with vowels

Abernathy	.A2	Ames	.A45	Astor	.A84
Adams	.A3	Appleby	.A6	Atwater	.A87
Aldrich	.A4	Archer	.A7	Austin	.A9

2 Names beginning with the letter S

Saint	.S2	Simmons	.S5	Steel	.S7
Schaefer	.S3	Smith	.S6	Storch	.S75
Seaton	.S4	Southerland	.S64	Sturges	.S8
Shank	.S45	Springer	.S66	Sullivan	.S9

3 Names beginning with the letters Qu

Qadriri	.Q2	Quick	.Q5	Qureshi	.Q7
Quabbe	.Q3	Queist	.Q6	Quynn	.Q9
Queener	.Q4				

4 Names beginning with other consonants—( ) = if using two numbers

Carter	.C3(7)	Cinelli	.C5(6)	Cullen	.C8(4)
Cecil	.C4(2)	Corbett	.C6(7)	Cyprus	.C9(6)
Childs	.C45	Croft	.C7(6)		

5 When there are no existing conflicting entries in the CATALOGUE the use of a third letter book number may be preferred

Cabot	.C3	Callahan	.C34	Carter	.C37
Cadmus	.C32	Campbell	.C35	Cavelli	.C38
Caffrey	.C33	Cannon	.C36	Cazalas	.C39

'The numbers are decimals, thus allowing for infinite interpolation of the decimal principle.

'Since the tables provide only a general framework for the assignment of numbers, the symbol for a particular name or work is constant only within a single class. Each entry must be added to the existing entries . . . in such a way as to preserve alphabetic order in accordance with Library of Congress FILING rules.'[4]

This CUTTER NUMBER section is reproduced with kind permission from Library of Congress Cataloging Service Bulletin Winter 1979.[9]

CUTTER NUMBERS FOR TRANSLATIONS
There are special cutters for translations, e.g.:

- 13 English
- 16 Italian

14 French
17 Russian

15 German
18 Spanish

Anweiler, Oskar

The soviets: the Russian workers,
peasants, and soldiers councils,
1905 – 1921. – New York : Pantheon
Books, 1975.

HX313.A513   Translation into
English of
Anweiler

RESERVED/OFFICIAL CUTTER NUMBERS
Some cutter numbers can be allocated to any LC CLASS NUMBER to indicate form, e.g.:

- .A1   SERIALS, periodicals
- .A3   Autobiography
- .A1 – .A5   Government publications.

Class P (Literature and language) has allocated cutter tables for individual authors.

EDITING (the creation of consistent catalogue records from centralized data, copy cataloguing)

(a) Check that the cataloguing copy matches the item to be catalogued, and follows AACR2. If it does not match, make the necessary changes to the copy. There may be differences in: edition, physical description, statement of extent etc.

If the item is the first part of a monograph multivolume work, make an open entry: e.g. Vol. 1– .

ADDED COPIES, CONTINUATIONS, SERIALS and NEW EDITIONS have special instructions.

If the item names more than three authors who have shared responsibility, enter the first named and add ... [et al.]

(b) Check the form of headings, both the MAIN HEADING and ADDED ENTRIES for consistency with the existing catalogue. The aim is to bring all works by one author together in the CATALOGUE. This may involve checking the AUTHORITY FILES and creating new headings.

If the author's name you are checking is not already in the catalogue, use its most commonly available form, e.g.:

- ELIOT, T S *not* ELIOT, Thomas Stearns.

In the case of a single author as MAIN HEADING in exactly the same form as in the book, there is no need to repeat it after the title in the catalogue entry.

Use conventional titles of CORPORATE BODIES, e.g.:

- DURHAM UNIVERSITY *not* UNIVERSITY OF DURHAM.

Alter the cataloguing copy to suit the catalogue's accepted forms of names. Check SUBJECT HEADINGS for consistency.

Delete any ADDED ENTRIES and LC CLASS NUMBERS in square brackets [ ] or marked DNLM (US National Library of Medicine), or those in foreign languages from contributing national cataloguing networks. However, *see* EXCEPTIONS TO LIBRARY OF CONGRESS for Class Z and SERIES.

(c)   Check that CUTTER NUMBERS are consistent with the catalogue, using the CUTTER TABLE if necessary to fit the new item into the alphabetical shelf sequence. Alter cataloguing copy to suit.

(d)   Some elements in cataloguing copy can be omitted according to current library practice and LEVEL OF DESCRIPTION adopted. However, where translators and illustrators have made a substantial contribution to the work, their names should not be left out.

      Items which may be omitted include: preliminary paging in Roman numerals, size, price, dates after authors' names (see AUTHOR MAIN HEADING), note of first edition, details of SERIES.

      Tables, charts, maps, graphs, etc., can all be abbreviated to 'ill.', or omitted altogether.

(e)   Notes should be kept to a minimum. They may include pages of a bibliography (lists of further reading), e.g.:

- Bibliography:p.159 – 162.

      Translation or reprint information can be included in a note, e.g.:

- First published in Paris 1932.

(f)   It may be necessary to add information to the cataloguing copy such as the ISBN and library circulation/control number.

(g)   Check the LC CLASS NUMBER on the copy and put it on the book verso title page. Any more than six characters on a line will need to be split in a logical fashion (to fit the average book spine label) as will decimal points, e.g.:

- PS3545.O337Z49 1988 becomes PS
                                         3545
                                         O337
                                         Z49
                                         1988

SPECIAL LOCATIONS are indicated in brackets at the beginning of the LC CLASS NUMBER, to help library users find what they want.

Dates of NEW EDITIONS, CONFERENCES etc. are added at the end.

(h) For manual catalogues you will need to calculate how many entries are required – shelflist, MAIN and ADDED ENTRIES (plus extra entries for any special catalogues).

Create correct number of entries.

(i) Send the item to PROCESSING.

EDITING CHECKLIST
(a) Does the cataloguing copy match the item being catalogued?
(b) Are the headings consistent with existing ones?
(c) Does the cutter number fit in the existing shelf order?
(d) What can be left out?
(e) What should be put in notes?
(f) What should be added?
(g) Mark LC number on the item and add it to the cataloguing copy.
(h) How many catalogue entries are required (manual catalogues)?
(j) Process the item.

EXCEPTIONS TO LIBRARY OF CONGRESS

Some specific items on LC cataloguing copy may need to be altered or omitted.

[CLASS K LAW]
LC was slow to produce a scheme for Law. One alternative is the Moys scheme which has a less American orientation and is shown in this handbook.

[CLASS Z BIBLIOGRAPHY, LIBRARY SCIENCE]
Use this class only for books on librarianship etc. Use the alternative LC CLASS NUMBER given for bibliographies on other subjects; where this is not given pass item to ORIGINAL CATA-LOGUING for classification. The alternative number is usually given in square brackets [ ].

[UNIFORM TITLES] (25.1–2)
These are titles usually printed in square brackets on cataloguing copy, for material which is translated into many languages or appears in several editions so that all editions file together in the catalogue. It is possible to delete uniform titles and catalogue the item in hand. However, a title in two languages linked by = indic-ates a work in two languages (parallel title) and these should be retained. References can be made from the second to the first title. (1.1D)

[SERIES CLASSIFICATION]
LC sometimes classifies books in SERIES. This can be rejected and an alternative number used for individual volumes if there is one, or provided originally. Series classification can be recognized by numbers appearing as part of the CUTTER NUMBER. The alternative number is usually given in square brackets [ ].

[VARIANT SPELLINGS] (1.0E1)
SUBJECT HEADINGS such as LABOR can be changed to LABOUR if absolutely necessary but the spelling used in the cata-

logue description must *not* be altered from that found in the book. Altering spelling can lead to a lack of consistency and potential filing difficulties.

Transliteration tables from LC can be used for items in a non-Roman alphabet. They are found in Library of Congress Cataloging Service Bulletin Summer 1976.[9]

FILING

LC Filing Rules (1980) should be used for filing catalogues.[4] These rules were particularly designed for computer filing and file entries exactly as they appear, e.g. Mc comes after Mac. The rules were also developed to emphasize the kind of headings prescribed by AACR2.

Points to remember are:

- file exactly as spelt, word by word and letter by letter
- accents are ignored
- numerals file at the start of the catalogue
- hyphenated words count as two words
- initials count as separate words
- 'a', 'an', 'the' ignored (except in E. European and Indic languages).

When, as sometimes occurs in filing, you find several apparently identical headings you should use the following arrangement:

- Personal forenames
- Personal surnames
- Place names
- Things (corporate body)
- Titles

SUBJECT HEADINGS
Follow LC Filing Rules (1980) Rule 5.7.[4]

Simple SUBJECT HEADINGS file in this order:

(a) SUBJECT HEADING
(b) SUBJECT HEADING – Subdivision
(c) SUBJECT HEADING, additional words
(d) SUBJECT HEADING (qualifier)
(e) SUBJECT HEADING as part of a phrase

Here is an example:

(a) Education
(b) Education – Costs
(c) Education, Higher
(d) Education (Christian theology)
(e) Education and state

Subject subdivisions file in this order:

(a) Period
(b) Form/topical
(c) Geographical

Here is an example:

(a) Education – 1945–1964
(b) Education – Research
(c) Education – United States

EXPLANATORY REFERENCES (scope notes)
File *before* entries with the same heading.

SEE ALSO REFERENCES (BT, NT, RT)
File *after* entries with the same heading.

INTERNATIONAL STANDARD BOOK NUMBERS (ISBN) (1.8B)

ISBNs are numeric codes uniquely identifying each published item and including information on the publisher. They were first introduced in 1967 and so will not be found on pre-1967 items. There are separate ISBNs for paperback and hardback editions of the same work, as well as for different publishers of the same work. ISBNs can be used for ordering books and finding cataloguing data for them. They should be added to cataloguing records whenever possible. They can be used as item control numbers in automated systems.

STRUCTURE OF ISBNs
Every ISBN consists of ten digits and may be quoted in computerized systems as a simple string of numbers, or it can be divided into four parts by dashes or spaces. The four parts of the number are made up as follows:

(a) Group identifier (national and/or language), e.g.:
- 0 or 1* UK, USA, Australia, Canada, New Zealand
- 2 France, French-speaking: Belgium, Canada, Switzerland
- 3 Austria, Germany, German-speaking Switzerland
- 4 Japan
- 5 USSR
- 7 China
- 91 Sweden
- 92 International organizations
- 958 Colombia
- 978 Nigeria.

* The identifier 1 is given to 'newer' publishers, e.g. 1 85057 for Magna Print Books.

(b) Publisher prefix, e.g.:
- 19 Oxford University Press
- 7043 The Women's Press.

N.B. The length of the publisher identifier is inversely proportionate to the output of the publisher (the same applies to the group identifier).

(c) Title identifier.

(d) Check digit. This is always the last digit, used by computer systems to validate the whole ISBN against transcription errors. Automated library order systems will check the validity of ISBNs. The check digit X denotes 10.

There is a similar system for SERIALS. International Standard Serial Numbers (ISSNs) are made up of two groups of four digits.

LEVELS OF DESCRIPTION (1.0D)

AACR2 provides for three levels of description when cataloguing. Level 3 (the highest level) includes every possible descriptive detail available in AACR2. Level 2 is the intermediate level and Level 1 is the basic level.

Level 1 is described as follows:

'Title proper / first statement of responsibility, if different from main entry in form or number or if there is no main entry heading. – Edition statement. – Material (or type of publication) specific details. – First publisher, etc., date of publication, etc. – Extent of item. – Note(s). – Standard number' (AACR2).

The terms used in this level of description are defined in a series of rules: 1.1B, 1.1F, 1.2B, 1.3, 1.4D, 1.4F, 1.5B, 1.7 and 1.8B.

The examples in this handbook generally follow Level 1 with the addition of first place of publication and simple series information. Libraries will differ in the level of description adopted for their catalogues but Level 1 should be viewed as a minimum. Also once a minimum standard has been agreed it must be adhered to for the sake of consistency.

PUNCTUATION AND LAYOUT OF ENTRIES is dealt with under a separate heading in this handbook.

LIBRARY OF CONGRESS CLASS NUMBERS (classification numbers, call numbers, shelf numbers, classmarks, shelf-marks)[11, 12]

The Library of Congress classification system was originally developed in 1898 for use only in the Library of Congress itself. It was based on the collection and proposed collection of that library and developed in a practical rather than a logical way. However, other libraries soon adopted the scheme and made use of the cataloguing data from such a large library (currently over 80 million volumes). It is widely used in American academic libraries. Basic class numbers are given with 40% of headings in LCSH.

The basic outline of LC is as follows:

- A   General works
- B   Philosophy and religion
- C   Auxiliary sciences of history (archaeology, genealogy etc.)
- D   History
- E–F History (America)
- G   Geography
- H   Social sciences
- J   Political sciences
- K   Law
- L   Education
- M   Music
- N   Fine arts
- P   Language and literature
- Q   Science
- R   Medicine
- S   Agriculture
- T   Technology
- U   Military science
- V   Naval science
- Z   Library science.

ARRANGEMENT OF LC CLASSIFICATION

The arrangement of the scheme is firstly by single capital letters, then by double and now in a few cases treble letters. As LC develops to include new subject areas, some class numbers begin with three letters, e.g. DJK History – Eastern Europe. This practice started in the Law schedules, class KF American Law, where a third letter indicates the state, e.g. KFC Californian State Law.

Changes in the schedules for each main class are given by complete new editions (T, for example, is now in its fifth edition) and further interim information is given in *LC classification – additions and changes.*[13]

Divisions and subdivisions within each class are shown by whole numbers in numerical order which can be extended decimally to add new areas; for example, the names of new computer programming languages.

- Q   Science
- QA   Mathematics
- QA76   Computer science
- QA76.7   Programming languages
- QA76.73   Individual languages

A24	ALGOL
C25	COBOL

There are still some potential main class letters available for expansion of the whole scheme.

Class numbers are then followed by author numbers called CUTTER NUMBERS. A date may follow the CUTTER to indicate a NEW EDITION or a CONFERENCE. In some areas, notably classes D and J, dates form a crucial part of the class number and must not be altered. They are part of the subject description of the item and not necessarily connected with its date of publication.

AUXILIARY TABLES IN LC

Several classes provide auxiliary tables for consistent subdivision of a section by geographical area, for example. Check which table (I, II, III ...) the schedules direct you to use. Find the relevant country number in the correct table. Add the country number to the one given at the foot of the page of the schedules you are consulting. Such subdivision tables appear at the end of each schedule before the index. This is usually a task for ORIGINAL CATALOGUING.

LC class numbers should appear in catalogue records in the same format as they appear on the spines of books otherwise library users will not be able to find the books they want. They should be split if necessary in a logical fashion with no more than six digits to a line (in order to fit on the spine label of the average book), e.g.:

Q	QA	QC	QC
7	76	73	73
H32	.4	F22	.8
	L52C29	1973	B29
		v.2	

If you need to record LC numbers in a horizontal fashion these examples would read:

- Q7.H32
- QA76.4.L52C29
- QC73.F22.1973v.2
- QC73.8.B29

Correct transcription of LC class numbers is crucial, in particular where an automated circulation system makes use of the numbers and a computer program validates them.

CLASS NUMBERS FOR MAPS

Sets of maps which are catalogued with open entries like CONTINUATIONS replace the date which would normally be part of the class number with a code indicating the scale of the maps. For example, a scale of 1:50,000 would be represented as s50. So the class number for an Ordnance Survey map in the first series could be G5740.s50.O72.

Despite the fact that triple CUTTER NUMBERS are apparently not permissible in LC, they sometimes appear on LC records for atlases.[8]

LIMBO (backlog, arrearage)

Books newly arrived in the library, and recently published, for which cataloguing copy cannot immediately be found, can be put in limbo. They can then be re-checked on the next cataloguing service update. If cataloguing copy is still not found, or they are urgently required in the meantime, they must pass to ORIGINAL CATALOGUING.

TEMPORARY CATALOGUE ENTRIES can be made for items in limbo to alert library users to their arrival in the library.

The increasing incidence of CIP information for books should cut down the number of books which are delayed in this manner. Conversely, this may also necessitate a longer delay in limbo for those books lacking cataloguing copy. Much depends on how much time is available for ORIGINAL CATALOGUING. In any event, books in limbo should be dealt with in order of receipt and not delayed unnecessarily.

MAIN HEADING (21.0, 21.1)

MANUAL CATALOGUE
A catalogue entry is produced for all items in the library with the choice of main heading according to AACR2. This can be either AUTHOR MAIN HEADING or TITLE MAIN HEADING. Several identical entries are produced for each item and then the required ADDED ENTRIES can be inserted across the top or highlighted in the tracings in card catalogues.

Here is an example of a complete set of entries for one book:

Main entry

> Dickinson, Henry W.
>   James Watt and the steam engine : the
>   memorial volume / prepared for the
>   committee of the Watt centenary commem-
>   oration at Birmingham 1919 by H.W.
>   Dickinson and Rhys Jenkins. –
>   Ashbourne : Moorland, 1981.
>   415p. : ill.
>
>   First published 1928.
>   Bibliography: p. 359 – 372.
>   ISBN 0 – 903485 – 92 – 3
>
>   1. Watt, James 1736 – 1819 2. Steam engineering
>   I. Title II. Jenkins, Rhys
>   TJ268.D53.1981

Subject headings added entries

> Watt, James 1736 – 1819
>
> Dickinson, Henry W.
>
>   James Watt and the steam engine . . . .
>
>   TJ268.D53.1981

```
┌─────────────────────────────────────────────────────────────┐
│         Steam engineering                                     │
│                                                              │
│         DICKINSON, Henry W.                                   │
│                                                              │
│              James Watt and the steam engine . . . .         │
│                        TJ268.D53.1981                        │
```

Author/title added entries

```
┌─────────────────────────────────────────────────────────────┐
│         James Watt and the steam engine                      │
│                                                              │
│         Dickinson, Henry W.                                   │
│                                                              │
│              James Watt and the steam engine . . . .         │
│                        TJ268.D53.1981                        │
```

```
┌─────────────────────────────────────────────────────────────┐
│         Jenkins, Rhys                                         │
│                                                              │
│         Dickinson, Henry W.                                   │
│                                                              │
│              James Watt and the steam engine . . . .         │
│                        TJ268.D53.1981                        │
```

ONLINE CATALOGUE

In online catalogues virtually all parts of an entry can act as access points for catalogue users. Because of this the concept of a main entry is of decreasing importance. However, one heading must still be chosen according to AACR2 in order to display records in a consistent manner.

MARCFICHE (Bibliofile)

Marcfiche is, as its name implies, a microfiche service providing MARC data, as released by the Library of Congress in Washington, and can therefore be a major source of cataloguing copy.[5] The Library of Congress acquires all significant items published in the USA and actively purchases other items from around the world. Marcfiche also contains COMARC data, i.e. that provided by other co-operating libraries such as the British Library. The primary coverage is English language titles since 1966, but it also contains both older and non-English titles. All new MARC data appears on Marcfiche, including NON-BOOK MATERIAL, maps, SERIALS and CIP entries.

The service consists of a main section of Library of Congress cataloguing which is added to weekly, a quarterly index and cumulative weekly indexes. The indexes can be searched by:

- LC card number
- ISBN
- AUTHOR/TITLE/MAIN HEADING
- LC CLASS NUMBER.

The index entries give the fiche number and position within the fiche for the entry you require. At any time you need only check in two places – the main index and the weekly index.

Filing in the Marcfiche indexes is letter by letter ignoring punctuation, which is treated as a space. 'A' and 'the' are ignored only in English. The index entries are truncated which means that a common title such as 'Introduction to ...' is not best approached via the title. However, in most cases title approach is very effective.

The fiche number you find is made up of three sections. For example, 1761415 means:

- cataloguing fiche number   1761
- column   4
- sequential position in column   15.

The columns are marked 1, 2, 3, 4, a, b, c ... z. Symbols are used in the index to indicate:

- *first occurrence in the update
- – CIP
- // first occurrence of CIP.

Every entry provides full cataloguing information (unless it is a CIP entry). A print can be taken from the fiche and the information used for EDITING to suit local requirements.

MARCFICHE EXAMPLES
The examples below show:

(a) – (d)   Marcfiche index entries
(e)   Marcfiche cataloguing entry
(f)   catalogue entry after editing.

The index entries are in the order in which they appear in Marcfiche. The examples are for Webster, Frank *The new photography.*

(a) *Marcfiche index entry: LC Card number (title)*

81-456786	Nuove tendenze : Milano e	1764y10
81-456787	The new photography : resp	1761415
81-456788	European colour photograph	1761416

(b) *Marcfiche index entry: ISBN (title)*

0-7145-3794-2	Traditions of the classica	1624d08
0-7145-3798-5	The new photography : resp	1761415
0-7145-3800-0	Journey to the end of the -	1535y26

(c) *Marcfiche index entry: (a) Author (main entry)*

Webster, Felicia.	*Library usage: a	018t17
Webster, Frank.	*The new photogra	1761415
Webster, Frederick E.	*Industrial marke	1336f24

Marcfiche index entry: (b) Title (added entry)

New photography Australia : a //	75-330133	544x10
The new photography : responsi //	81-456787	1761415
The new Phrynichus. Being a re //	72-384609	171n18

(d) *Marcfiche index entry: LC CLASS NUMBER (title)*

TR183.T87 1980	Guida alla critica fo	1736504
TR183.W42 1980	The new photography	1761415
TR185.A48 1980	Photo topics and tech-	1659q32

(e) *Marcfiche cataloguing entry*

------------------------------------1761415------------------------------------

Webster, Frank.
   The new photography : responsibility in visual communication /
by Frank Webster. London : J. Calder, 1980.
   viii, 262 p. : ill. ; 23 cm. (A Platform book)
   Includes bibliographical references and index.
   1. Photography – Social aspects.
I. Title.
ISBN 0-7145-3798-5
TR183.W42 1980   770'.1   81-456787

(f) *Catalogue entry after EDITING from Marcfiche*

Webster, Frank

The new photography : responsibility in
visual communication. – London : J. Calder,
1980.
   262p. : ill. – (A Platform book)

ISBN 0 – 7145 – 3798 – 5

1. Photography – Social aspects I. Title

TR183.W42

BIBLIOFILE
The same data as Marcfiche provides is also available on CD-ROM
under the name *Bibliofile*.[5]

NAME AUTHORITIES (22.1)

This quarterly cumulative LC service available on microfiche and CD-ROM is the major authority to use when deciding on the form of a name on which there is some doubt and for which there is no precedent in the CATALOGUE.[1] From the information found in Name Authorities, entries can be made for the AUTHORITY FILES. SUBJECT HEADINGS for proper names not found in LCSH can be set up. The form of heading for CONFERENCES can also be checked.

There are three types of entry in Name Authorities:

(a) Authority records which contain the full form of established heading including UNIFORM TITLES:
- a medium designator, e.g. VR videorecording
- the sources used (and not useful) for its establishment
- indication that the entry is an ADDED ENTRY or SUBJECT HEADING
- references needed with the heading:
  - x   see
  - xx   see also
- conformity with AACR2
- control data for LC including LC card number, date of heading establishment.

(b) Cross references: these are the references which direct library users from one form of heading to another:
- x   'see' references refer from unused to established headings
- xx   'see also' references refer to related headings, for example from SUBJECT HEADINGS to related personal headings.

(c) Information/history notes: these headings show, for example, where a corporate body has changed its name over time, directing users to earlier or later headings.

NAME AUTHORITIES – EXAMPLES

(a) *An established heading*

Webster, Frank.
Found:
His The new photography, 1980: t.p. (Frank Webster)
jkt. (Dr., sen. lect. in sociology at Oxford
Polytechnic)
AACR 2
DLC 10 – 24 – 80   n80 – 144215

(b) *Cross references*

BBC
see
British Broadcasting Corporation.

(c) *Information/history notes and related established heading*

British Broadcasting Company
see also the later heading
British Broadcasting Corporation.

British Broadcasting Corporation
see also the earlier heading
British Broadcasting Company.

The British Library produces a similar monthly cumulating
microfiche service called *Name Authority List*.[14] This is particularly
useful for UK libraries using MARC since it gives UKMARC
coding for names.

NATIONAL UNION CATALOG (NUC)[6]

Until 1982 this was an alphabetical printed catalogue by author (editor) and title. It was originally printed from reduced and reproduced catalogue cards from LC and other contributing (union) American libraries. In book form, it is a source of cataloguing copy for pre-1966 imprints. The information can be printed, photographed, photocopied or copied manually to create CATALOGUE ENTRIES, although some alterations may need to be made, e.g. changing an editor MAIN HEADING to a TITLE MAIN HEADING.

When checking NUC it must be remembered that the dates on the NUC volumes are the dates of the cataloguing of the book by LC and the other contributing libraries. Therefore, if you are checking a book published in 1966, it is worth checking both 1963–7 and 1968–72. Information transcribed from NUC can then go on to EDITING.

The example below shows a typical NUC entry with ADDED ENTRIES. There is usually a Dewey number and an LC card number, as well as the LC CLASS NUMBER.

> **Moran, Joan May.**
> Movement experiences for the mentally retarded or emotionally disturbed child ₍by₎ Joan May Moran ₍and₎ Leonard Harris Kalakian. Minneapolis, Burgess Pub. Co. ₍1974₎
> ix, 387 p. illus. 24 cm.
> Includes bibliographies.
> 1. Mentally handicapped children—Care and treatment—United States. 2. Movement, Psychology of. 3. Play therapy. I. Kalakian, Leonard H., joint author. II. Title.
> RJ501.A2M67   613.7′1′0240816   73–83575
> ISBN 0-8087-1359-0   MARC

Since 1982, NUC BOOKS has been produced on microfiche (COM) and is also available online and on CD-ROM. The complete record for a book on the microfiche is available in the register which has indexes by name, title, subject and series. The index entries are brief but may be sufficient for building a catalogue record. New entries for the register are added monthly and there are cumulative monthly indexes. NUC BOOKS contains records for: books, pamphlets, manuscripts, atlases, monographic microforms and government publications. It uses LC FILING rules for the indexes.

There are other NUC series for specific materials such as: NUC Audiovisual Materials and NUC Cartographic Materials.

NEW BOOKS

Deal with a batch of new books together.

(a) Check whether books need to be put into SPECIAL LOCATIONS, e.g. (Ref). Add this to the cataloguing copy and mark it in the book.

(b) CONTINUATIONS, NEW EDITIONS and ADDED COPIES can be removed for their own special treatment, as can SERIALS.

(c) Cataloguing copy (MARCFICHE, CIP, NUC, BIE etc.) should be found for the remaining items which can then be passed to EDITING. This is known as copy cataloguing.

(d) Very newly published books can await re-checking on the next cataloguing service update and remain until then in LIMBO.

(e) The remainder of the items without cataloguing copy are for ORIGINAL CATALOGUING in-house and this should be done according to AACR2, with LC CLASS NUMBERS and SUBJECT HEADINGS allocated.

The following flow chart demonstrates the movement of items through cataloguing: showing the checks for cataloguing data through to the production of a catalogue record.

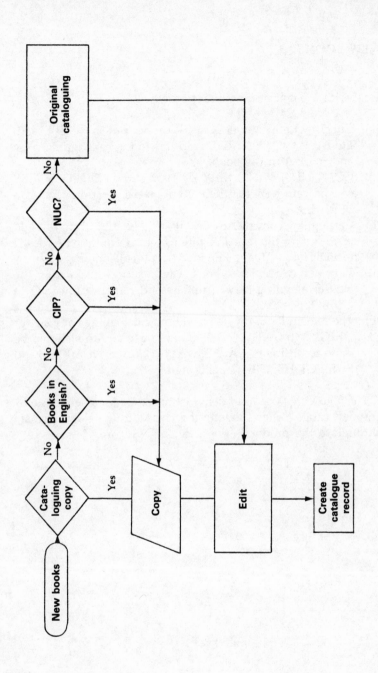

46

NEW EDITIONS (of items already in stock) (1.2)

EDITING THE CATALOGUE RECORD

(a) Using previous LC CLASS NUMBER add the publication date of the new edition at the end of the number.

(b) Alter description of the item for a catalogue entry to suit the new edition. You may have to alter the edition statement, publisher details, statement of extent, notes, ISBN.

(c) Check ADDED ENTRIES for authors, editors and title. There may be new authors or editors requiring mention in the catalogue. SUBJECT HEADINGS can generally remain the same.

(d) Write CLASS NUMBER on verso title page with edition date at end.

(e) Send item to PROCESSING and generate CATALOGUE ENTRIES.

Example of catalogue entries for three editions of the same work

Maudsley, Ronald Harling

Land law : cases and materials / by R.H. Maudsley and E.H. Burn. – 3rd ed. – London : Butterworths, 1975.
    882p.

ISBN 0-406-62304-X

1. Real property – Great Britain I. Title
II. Burn, E.H.
                                KN61.M38.1975

If there is more than one edition of a work in a single year, LC uses lower case letters a, b, c ... after the edition date to order them.

(LC often puts the publication date after the LC CLASS NUMBER for the first edition. This can be omitted.)

NON-BOOK MATERIAL (Chapters 3 – 11)

The 1988 revision of AACR2 gives detailed rules for the description of items which are not books:

• maps	Chapter 3
• manuscripts	Chapter 4
• music	Chapter 5
• sound recordings	Chapter 6
• films and videos	Chapter 7
• graphic materials	Chapter 8
• computer files	Chapter 9
• realia (3 dimensional objects)	Chapter 10
• microforms	Chapter 11.

For all these types of material the choice of headings follows the rules for books. Classification and SUBJECT HEADINGS are also similar except that SUBJECT HEADINGS may include a subdivision denoting the material type, e.g.:

- (i) France – Maps
- (ii) Economics – Computer programs
- (iii) Tunnels – Drawings
- (iv) Railroads – Songs and music.

The major differences in describing items which are not books are that a general or specific material designation should be given and the 'extent of item' is less likely to be a number of pages or volumes. Here are some examples:

- (i) atlas (57 leaves)
- (ii) computer disk
- (iii) 12 technical drawings : blueprint
- (iv) vocal score (10p.).

ORIGINAL CATALOGUING (1.0B1)

Original cataloguing is the creation of catalogue records for items where cataloguing copy cannot be found in any of the centralized sources. These items are sometimes known as EMMA (Extra MARC MAterial).

A standard CATALOGUE INPUT FORM can be used, as the example shows, to determine conformity of catalogue records. Online records can be input directly.

The description of the item should be given according to AACR2. Basically this entails:

- Describing the item (*see* EDITING)
- MAIN HEADING
- Title/statement of responsibility (using the best known form of names)
- Edition
- Material/type
- Publication (place: publisher, date)
- Extent (pagination or number of volumes or estimate ca.)
- [Illustrations]
- Series
- Notes, e.g. Bibliography:p.210 – 220
- ISBN
- LC SUBJECT HEADINGS
- ADDED ENTRIES.

PUNCTUATION AND LAYOUT for catalogue entries is shown later. Each item should be given an LC CLASS NUMBER and CUTTER NUMBER. Entries may need to be made in the AUTHOR/SERIES AUTHORITY FILES.

You will also have to record how many catalogue entries need to be made for a manual catalogue plus any special catalogues. The circulation or control number should be recorded as part of the catalogue record.

[PAMPHLETS] (1.0A2, 2.5B18)

Individual pamphlets can be classified in a simplified way, as shown in the examples below, at the start of the relevant class. Given separate CUTTER NUMBERS, they are brought together on the shelves in a box marked with the LC CLASS NUMBER. Government publications in pamphlet form can be put into a '00' sequence with running numbers rather than CUTTER NUMBERS if preferred.

Sometimes several pamphlets are bound together and in this case the term 'pamphlets' can be used in the statement of extent.

The examples show a pamphlet and a government publication.

Ashton, Thomas S.

Changes in the standards of comfort in eighteenth-century England. – London : British Academy, 1955.
16p. – (Raleigh lecture on history).

Offprint from British Academy proceedings 1955, p.171 – 187.

I. Title II. Series 1. Great Britain – History – 18th century

HD0.A83

Great Britain. Treasury

Treasury minute on the first special report and seventh to twelfth reports from the Committee of Public Accounts, 1987 – 88. – London: HMSO, 1988.
11p. – (Command papers; cm 323)

ISBN 0-10-103232-3

I. Title II. Series 1. Finance, public – Accounting – Great Britain

HJ00.no.12

PROCESSING

The work of processing library items involves labelling etc. so that they are clearly identifiable as belonging to the library. The LC CLASS NUMBER is printed or typed onto a label which is stuck onto the book's spine. It must exactly match the catalogue record or the item will be lost.

This is the stage at which circulation numbers can be inserted in books for whichever system is in use, and linked into any automated system with the required details.

Security triggers may also be inserted, and activated if necessary.

When a book is donated to the library, a label is usually fixed inside the front cover with the donor's name.

New library acquisitions can be displayed for library users.

Some processing work such as book jacketing, insertion of security triggers and bar-coding for circulation can be carried out by library suppliers before the book reaches the library. This will improve the chances of library users getting the books quickly.

PUNCTUATION AND LAYOUT (1.0C)

CATALOGUE ENTRIES should follow the layout as shown in the examples in this handbook. In some cases, where the description of an item is very long, it may be necessary to use two cards, or two screens on a computer terminal.

PUNCTUATION
The punctuation for catalogue description prescribed by AACR2 is as follows:

Title : subtitle / author's name ; names of other authors. – edition. – place of publication : publisher, year.
   physical description. – (series)
   note(s).
   ISBN

Precede each area, other than the first area, by a full stop, space, dash, space (. –) unless the area begins a new paragraph.
Data taken from outside prescribed sources is put in square brackets [ ].

Example:

Taylor, Lance

Macro models for developing countries. –
London : McGraw-Hill, 1979.
   271p. – (Economics handbooks series)

Includes bibliographies.
ISBN 0-07-063135-2

1. Developing countries 2. Economic
development – Mathematical models
3. Macroeconomics – Mathematical models
I. Title II. Series

        HC59.7.T39

CAPITALIZATION *(Appendix A)*

Capitals are used in all entries in this handbook for first letters of names, e.g. publishers, ADDED ENTRIES for authors.

AUTHOR MAIN HEADING – capitals are used for surnames and initials or first letters of forenames. Capitals are used for the first letter of the title.

TITLE MAIN HEADING – Capitals are used for the first letter of the title and for the first letter of the definite or indefinite article which may precede it.

N.B. Different cataloguing agencies will have different capitalization practices. In general, the trend is away from extensive use of upper case characters for the whole of a heading. However consistency in cataloguing is crucial in order to help library users looking for books.

SERIALS (12.0)

The term 'serial' is used to cover periodicals, newspapers, journals, serials, annuals, regularly published proceedings etc.

Serials can be classified by LC, as are books and other items. The designation .A1 can be used practically anywhere in the LC classification when no provision for serials is provided under a topic.

If entries are made in the CATALOGUE they may carry a SPECIAL LOCATIONS designation for serials.

A sample AACR2 catalogue entry for a serial is shown below.

> Journal of social policy. – Vol. 1, pt. 1
> (Jan.1972). – London: Cambridge University
> Press, 1972 –
>   Quarterly
>   Library holdings v.1 –
>
> ISSN 0047-2794
>
> 1. Social policy – Periodicals 2. Great Britain –
> Social policy – Periodicals
> (Per)HV1.J57

LC CLASS NUMBERS for serials can be found in directories such as the *Serials directory* from Ebsco as well as in NUC.[15]

The listing of serials can be made in a separate SERIALS list showing:

- TITLE   LIBRARY HOLDINGS   (LOCATION) CLASS NUMBER

This type of listing can easily be stored in a computer and printed out when required. The following is a section of Brunel University Library's Journals List.

CHILD POVERTY ACTION GRP.J.	5-	1967-	HV245.A1P6
CHILD WELFARE	51-	1972	HV741.A1C3
CHILD WELFARE LEAGUE AM.J.	51-	1972-	HV741.A1C3
CHILDREN	18-	1971-	HV741.A1C5
CHILDREN TODAY	1-	1972-	HV741.A1C53
CHINA Q.	27-	1966-	DS701.C46
CHINA YB.	CURRENT YEAR ONLY		DS895.F68C54

SERIES (21.30L)

A series is a collection of items which, while they may have individual authors and titles, belong to a group which carries a series title. Individual items within the series usually have a number. Sometimes there is more than one series involved. CONFERENCES are often part of a series. Not to be confused with CONTINUATIONS, which are multi-volume works – for example, the collected works of an author. Nor to be confused with SERIALS, which appear regularly in parts.

(a) Record series information after the statement of extent (pagination).
Number in the series is recorded after a semi-colon (;), e.g.:

- (British Library information guide; 5)

N.B. The important factor to consider is whether the series information will be useful as an ADDED ENTRY to library users – what AACR2 calls a 'useful collocation'.

(b) If the series is simply a publisher's device to attract sales or to indicate similar physical features, do not make a series ADDED ENTRY. For example:

- (Routledge pocket books)
- (Berg women's series)

(c) If the series is well known or likely to be sought by library users, make an ADDED ENTRY. For example:

- (German historical perspectives)
- (New horizons in therapeutics)

(d) If in doubt, make a series ADDED ENTRY.

(e) Keep an AUTHORITY FILE of all series headings so that library policy is consistent. It is not helpful to record only some items in a series.
Use NAME AUTHORITIES[1] to check form of series name.

(f) Avoid SERIES CLASSIFICATION which may appear on cataloguing copy. This may bring together disparate subjects on the shelves or, at the least, generalize a complex topic.

SHELVING

Arrange items in the library according to their LC CLASS NUMBERS.

This is achieved by taking the first letter on the left,

- then the second letter if there is one
- then the third letter if there is one
- then the whole number following (these numbers are not decimal)
- then the decimal number(s) following the point if there are any
- then the alphabetical letter followed by a number(s) – CUTTER NUMBERS (CUTTER NUMBERS are decimal numbers).

For shelving purposes ignore copy numbers.

Where a work consists of several volumes these should be put in order.

Different editions of one work should be put in order.

An item wrongly shelved is lost to library users and staff alike.

Here is an example of LC shelving order:

Q	Q	QC	QC	QC	QC	QC	QC	QC	QC
7	77	7	73	73	73	73	73	73	73
H32	B71	H32	.4	.4	.6	.8	.8	.8	.8
			B62	B75	B62	B62	B62	F22	F22
						v.1	v.2	1967	1973

SPECIAL LOCATIONS

It is often necessary for libraries to have special areas reserved for particular categories of items. The location symbols only indicate a particular location for items in the library and can be ignored when filing the catalogue, although they may also have their own separate catalogues. Sequences can be combined, e.g. (A/V)(Ref).

The more locations that are devised the harder it is for library users to find the items they want. Here are some possible special locations.

- (Ref)   Reference books, dictionaries, encyclopaedias
- (Ab)   Abstracts, indexes, bibliographies
- (Qto)   Quarto books too big to fit on the normal shelves
- (A/V)   Audio-visual materials
- (GOV) Government publications
- (Per)   Periodicals, annuals, SERIALS, regular proceedings, journals.

Jefferies, John

A guide to the official publications of the European Communities . . .

(Ab)HC241.2.J44

THE Next whole earth catalog :
access to tools / edited by Stewart Brand . . .

(Ref)HC155.W56

Ormond, Richard

The face of monarchy : British royalty portrayed . . .

(Qto)DA28.1.O75

SUBJECT HEADINGS[16]: Introduction

Setting up subject headings can be done as and when books are catalogued and a list of requirements is made for headings new to the catalogue, or this can be done at the EDITING stage. Online cataloguing systems may have LCSH available online, and then there is no need to set up the reference structure. However, it is as well to know how it operates.

Headings are listed in bold type in LCSH and may have two initial instructions. (*May Subd Geog*) indicates that a heading can be subdivided by place. (*Not Subd Geog*) means the opposite. Forty per cent of the headings also carry LC class numbers showing the most general occurrence of the topic in the schedules. Scope notes are given with some headings to ensure consistent application. Here is an example:

Heading —▶ **Amateur plays** (*May Subd Geog*) ◀— can be subdivided by place

LC class no.—▶ [*PN 6119.9*]

scope note {
Here are entered collections of plays, skits, recitations, etc. for production by nonprofessionals. Works about, including history and criticism of, such plays are entered under Amateur theater.
}

LC class numbers may differ for different aspects of one subject, and this is often indicated, for example:

- **Mouth** [*QL 857 (Anatomy)*]
  [*QM 306 (Human anatomy)*]

SETTING UP SUBJECT HEADINGS
(a) Deal with each subject heading separately
(b) If it is already on file do nothing
(c) If not on file, check LCSH. If not found in LCSH check NAME AUTHORITIES[1]
(d) Create reference structure as described below.

SUBJECT HEADINGS: Reference structure (Cross references)

Most subject headings carry instructions for creating cross references. The symbols used have been introduced to help library users to understand the relationship between headings. The symbols are:

- BT   broader term (see also from)
- NT   narrower term (see also)
- RT   related term
- SA   see also (general reference)
- UF   used for (rejected heading)
- USE   use instead (preferred heading).

Below is an example of a heading with the references which are prescribed to be used with it:

- **Criminal law** *(May Subd Geog)*

UF	Crimes and misdemeanors Felony Law, Criminal Penal law	Use for
BT	Pleas of the crown Public law	Broader terms
RT	Criminal procedure Punishment	Related terms
SA	*subdivision* Criminal provisions *under legal topics, e.g.* Corporation law – Criminal provisions	General references
NT	Abduction Accomplices Adoption – Corrupt practices Adultery	Narrower terms

SUBJECT HEADINGS: USE references

If a subject heading is followed by USE this indicates that the term you have looked for is rejected and the preferred term or form is listed after USE. For example:

- Chapbooks ◄──────────── rejected form of heading
    USE Chap-books ◄─────── preferred heading

If you look up Chap-books you will find:

- **Chap-books** ◄──────────── preferred heading
    UF Chapbooks ◄─────── used instead of (for)

This is then the authority record. The public catalogue must contain a reference for users who look up Chapbooks to direct them to Chap-books:

- Chapbooks USE Chap-books.

If preferred, the word SEE can be used in place of USE. However, the terms used to indicate reference relationships in LCSH are commonly recognized terms now found in thesauri (lists of prescribed subject headings incorporating a reference structure). If you are using LCSH online it would be sensible not to change any of the terms used.

USE references often occur where a heading is made up of more than one word, to make clear which part of the heading is the filing element:

- Schools, community USE Community schools.

USE references can also be added for preferred spellings if necessary:

- Colour USE Color

or if you simply want to make clear which is the preferred heading where there might be some doubt about the spelling used.

Since 1985 LC has linked subject headings by cross references shown as BT (Broader Term) and NT (Narrower Term). These references imply a hierarchical or ranked relationship moving from the general to the specific, from the broader term to the narrower term.

A heading which appears as a BT (Broader term) will also appear elsewhere as the NT (Narrower term) in LCSH. For example:

- **Easter cookery** ◄─────────── the library has this topic
    BT Holiday cookery ◄─────────── the library has this topic

. . . .

  Holiday cookery ◄─────────── the library has this topic
    [TX739]
    BT   Cookery ◄─────────── the library has this topic
       Holidays ◄─────────── the library does not have this
       Christmas cookery ◄─── the library does not have this
    NT   Easter cookery ◄─── the library does have this topic
       Hanukkah cookery ◄─── the library does not have this
       Passover cookery ◄─── the library does not have this
       Thanksgiving cookery ◄─ the library does not have this

This heading shows that **Easter cookery** is only a narrow part of a subject grouping which includes all types of cooking for holidays (**Holiday cookery**). **Holiday cookery** is a broad term which can include cooking for various holidays, i.e. Christmas, Easter, Hanukkah, Passover, Thanksgiving. **Holiday cookery** is is itself part of the broader headings **Cookery** and **Holidays**. The rank or hierarchy is moving from the general to the more specific:

- Cookery .... Holiday cookery .... Easter cookery.

The catalogue should include only references for which the library has stock. There is no point in making a reference to a topic which is not covered in the library. The example given above, bearing in mind which topics are covered in the library, would prompt the following entries for the catalogue:

- Easter cookery   BT   Holiday cookery

  . . . . .

  Holiday cookery   BT   Cookery

  . . . . .

  Holiday cookery   NT   Easter cookery

There would be no references to Holidays, Christmas cookery, Hanukkah cookery, Passover cookery or Thanksgiving cookery as these topics are not represented in the library stock.

Such relationships can be shown in the catalogue by linking headings with the symbols BT and NT, so long as they are clearly explained in catalogue instructions. If there is no symbol key, BT and NT must be spelled out as Broader Term and Narrower Term. Some libraries display the 'big red books' but the symbols will still need to be explained in order to help library users to define a search.[16]

Before 1985, these relationships between headings would have been expressed simply with the linking phrase 'see also' (xx and sa in authority files). The new terms BT and NT allow the library user to make a catalogue search broader or narrower as required.

The symbol RT in LCSH is used to link two related headings which are associated, but do not form part of a rank or hierarchy (BT and NT). The symbol RT is not used very frequently.

● **Deformations (Mechanics)**
   RT   Rheology ◄─────────── the library has this topic
        Strains and stresses ◄── the library does not have this

References to related terms prompted by the above would require the following in the catalogue:

● Deformations   RT   Rheology
   . . . . .
   Rheology   RT   Deformations

There would be no references to **Strains and stresses** as this is not covered in the library.

[*GENERAL REFERENCES*]
General references (SA) are given in LCSH where a whole group of headings can be individually differentiated if covered by the library. For example:

               Degrees, Academic ◄──── the library has this topic
                  SA   *names of specific degrees e.g.*
the library ──►Bachelor of arts degree, Doctor of
has this topic   philosophy degree ◄──── the library does
                                              not have this

The following references would be needed in the catalogue:

● Bachelor of arts degree   BT   Degrees, Academic
   . . . . .
   Degrees, Academic   SA   Bachelor of arts degree.

There would be no reference to **Doctor of philosophy degree** as the library does not have this topic.

Complex subjects in LCSH can be represented by combining different concepts to create a single heading. Some of the subdivisions which may be used are printed in LCSH but by no means all. The Subject Cataloguing Manual gives the rules for assigning subdivisions.[17]

Subdivisions are shown following headings and a long dash. Two long dashes indicate the use of two subdivisions. For example:

- **Dams**
  - Design and construction
  - Foundations
  - Inspection
  - — Law and legislation

This shows that you can use the following subject headings in the catalogue:

- Dams — Design and construction
  Dams — Foundations
  Dams — Inspection
  Dams — Inspection — Law and legislation

TOPICAL SUBDIVISIONS
Topical subdivisions are added to subject headings to clearly limit the main heading, for example:

- Econometrics – Computer programs

This heading implies that the work being catalogued is concerned with computer programs used in econometrics, rather than being a general work on econometrics.

Topical subdivisions can generally be added to main headings and the rules for their application and a comprehensive list of such subdivisions will be found in the manual.[17] They are not printed out in LCSH every time they are applicable.

Form subdivisions are used to show the physical or structural form of the material being catalogued. They can generally be used with any subject heading and are seldom printed in LCSH, although a general reference to their use may be found. For example:

- **Dictionaries, Polyglot**

  . . . . .
  > SA *subdivision* Dictionaries — Polyglot
  > *under topical subjects and*
  > *individual languages, e.g. English*
  > *language — Dictionaries — Polyglot*

  This shows that the subdivision

- Dictionaries – Polyglot

can be used under any language or subject, for example:

- **Chemistry, Physical and theoretical**

can be subdivided as:

- Chemistry, Physical and theoretical — Dictionaries — Polyglot

  Examples of form subdivisions are:
  — Abstracts
  — Congresses
  — Dictionaries
  — Handbooks, manuals, etc.
  — Illustrations
  — Periodicals
  — Statistics
  — Yearbooks.

A complete list of form and topical subdivisions which can be used as 'free-floating subdivisions' will be found in the manual.[17]

Chronological or period subdivisions are added to subject headings, (and to subject headings with other subdivisions already in place) to limit the subject clearly to a particular time period. Chronological subdivisions are almost always printed in LCSH with the heading which can be divided into time periods. Albanian history is an example:

- **Albania**
  - **History**
  - − − **To 1501**
  - − − **Turkish wars, 15th century**
  - − − **1501 – 1912**
  - − − **1878 – 1912**
  - − − **Uprising, 1912**
  - − − **1912 – 1944**
  - − − **Axis occupation, 1939 – 1944**
  - − − **1944 –**

As will be seen from this example, some of the periods allocated overlap and must therefore be allocated as subject headings carefully. Historical periods are specific to each region or country and *cannot* be re-applied elsewhere.

Some chronological subdivisions do not follow the common subdivision:

− History

When this is the case, the possible periods to be used will be printed:

- **Art, Japanese**
  - − To 794
  - − To 1600
  - − To 1868

If a subject heading or subject heading with subdivision is followed by the designation (*May Subd Geog*), this indicates that a geographical location may be added. For example:

● **Education** (*May Subd Geog*)

can be subdivided for items concerning education in various countries or regions. If the geographic subdivision is a country (or a larger area) it directly follows the subject heading. For example:

● **Education — Africa**
● **Education — Greece**

If the geographic subdivision required is smaller than a country, then the country name is interposed first. For example:

● Education — Greece — Athens.

However, if the smaller geographic subdivision is in:

(a) United States
(b) Great Britain
(c) Canada
(d) Soviet Union

the country name need not be interposed first. You can use respectively:

(a) The State, e.g. Texas
(b) The Constituent country, e.g. Scotland
(c) The Province, e.g. Ontario
(d) The Republic, e.g. Uzbekistan

to produce the following type of subject heading:

● Education – Wales
● Education – California – San Diego

Very few geographic subdivisions are printed in LCSH and the manual will provide the rules for their construction.[17] Examples are given in LCSH under France, Great Britain and United States.

SUBJECT HEADINGS: Subdivisions – Topical and Form and Geographic

Some subject headings can be subdivided geographically as well as by topic or form. In these cases it is crucial to take note of where the instruction (*May Subd Geog*) is given. Generally, the geographic subdivision follows the last element which can be subdivided by place. For example:

- **Computers** (*May Subd Geog*)
  — Access control
  — Study and teaching (*May Subd Geog*)
  — — Law and legislation (*May Subd Geog*)

could provide for the following type of headings:

- Computers — Australia
- Computers — Australia — Access control
- Computers — Study and teaching — Australia
- Computers — Study and teaching — Law and legislation — Australia.

In other words, the designation (*May Subd Geog*) indicates that the topic takes precedence; the place follows the topic.

If, however, the designation (*Not Subd Geog*), which is mostly used with family names, or no designation appears, or a general reference appears, then place takes precedence; the place precedes the subject. For example:

(a) **Elsevier family** (*Not Subd Geog*)
(b) **Devotional calendars**
(c) **Constitutional law**
  Here are entered works discussing constitutions
  . . . . . particular regions,
  countries, etc. are entered under the name of the place with the subdivision Constitutional law.

can provide for the following headings:

(a) Holland — Genealogy (family names require location headings)
(b) Holland — Devotional calendars
(c) Holland — Constitutional law

SUBJECT HEADINGS: Pattern headings (topical/form sub-divisions)

LCSH provides for standardized sets of topical and form subdivisions to be used for the subdivision of categories of headings. However, these are printed in LCSH only where the allocated pattern or model heading is provided.

If, for example, you are allocating subject headings for a book about an individual literary author, you can find all the possible subdivisions for authors under the Pattern heading:

- **Shakespeare, William 1564 – 1616**

There you will find six pages of possible subdivisions for authors.

A table of pattern headings for categories of subject is given in the introduction to LCSH and in the manual.[15, 16] Some of the more common categories allocated pattern headings are as follows:

Category	Pattern Heading
Animals	Fishes
Chemicals	Copper
Diseases	Cancer
Industries	Construction industry
Languages	English language
Legal topics	Labor laws and legislation
Literary authors	Shakespeare, William 1564 – 1616
Materials	Metals
Musical instruments	Piano
Organs and regions of the body	Heart
Plants and crops	Corn
Sacred works	Bible
Sports	Soccer

Guidecards can be made for a manual CATALOGUE, which means that it is not necessary to type separate headings across the top of each subject card. However, the relevant tracing on the card will have to be highlighted, to show the filing element.

Guidecards are catalogue cards 0.5cm taller than normal cards, preferably of a distinctive colour or with a coloured cover. Subject headings can be typed on them showing either headings or rejected headings. They are particularly suitable when there are scope notes or LC CLASS NUMBERS with subject entries. For example:

```
┌──────────────────────────────────────────────────────┐
│                Quantum chemistry                       │
└──────────────────────────────────────────────────────┘
```

```
┌──────────────────────────────────────────────────────┐
│                Chemistry, quantum                      │
     USE
     Quantum chemistry
```

The guidecards file before any catalogue entries with the same heading. If a subject heading is changed, you need only make a new guidecard and move the relevant SUBJECT entries with it (leaving a USE reference guidecard) to the new position.

71

TEMPORARY CATALOGUE ENTRIES

Temporary or skeleton entries should be made for books for which there will be some delay in completing cataloguing. This may happen with:

- Books on order
- New books in LIMBO
- Books which are borrowed immediately upon arrival in the library which will need more extensive cataloguing on return from loan. (Not a practice to be recommended.)
- Books put immediately into stock because of urgent need for which the cataloguing copy has been delayed.
- Books being re-classified. In this case it is important to put some sort of temporary entry in the CATALOGUE, in order to avoid duplicate CUTTER NUMBERS.
- Books awaiting ORIGINAL CATALOGUING.

Below is an example of a temporary entry for the catalogue:

Posener, Jill
Louder than words
Pandora, 1986
ON ORDER 17.7.90
Please fill out a reservation if you
would like to see this book
when it arrives.

THESES AND DISSERTATIONS (2.7B13)

Theses and dissertations are catalogued according to the provisions of AACR2. They have CUTTER NUMBERS and can be classified in a simplified way like PAMPHLETS. An identifier at the top of the LC CLASS NUMBER can indicate a thesis in the CATALOGUE since most libraries keep theses in a SPECIAL LOCATION. The class number is effectively the degree for which the thesis was prepared. Pagination is usually in leaves rather than pages, unless the thesis is published, in which case it can be catalogued like an ordinary book. The 'material type' must show the level of work and the institution.

Claiborne, Brenda Jean
Histamine as a putative neurotransmitter
in the lobster stomatogastric nervous
system, 1981.
  169 leaves. –
Thesis (DPhil) (Biochemistry) – Oxford
University, 1981

1. Lobsters – Physiology 2. Histamine –
Physiology I. Title II. Oxford University –
Thesis (DPhil.) (Biochemistry:1981)

Thesis D.Phil.C43

TITLE MAIN HEADING (21.1C)

The title is used as MAIN HEADING when an item has no obvious author(s), is an edited collection of contributions, e.g. CONFERENCE, handbook, reader, religious scripture; or has more than three authors. In the latter case there will also be ADDED ENTRIES for first named authors and the conventional ... [et al.] put after the first author's name in the description. Pre-AACR2 headings will need to be altered in cataloguing copy for CONFERENCES and edited works. The examples below show an edited collection and a work by more than three authors.

The rights and wrongs of
   women / edited and introduced by
   Juliet Mitchell and Ann Oakley. –
   Harmondsworth : Penguin, 1976.
      438p. –

ISBN 0-14-021616-2

1. Women's rights – Addresses, essays,
lectures 2. Feminism – Addresses, essays,
lectures I. Mitchell, Juliet (ed.) II. Oakley, Ann (ed.)

HQ1154.R54

South America : river trips / by
   Richard Bangs ... [et al.]. – Cambridge,
   Mass. : Bradt, 1981 –
      v.1- : ill.

ISBN 0-933982-13-5

1. South America – Description and travel
2. Rivers – South America – Guide-books
I. Bangs, Richard

F2211.S67

[DESIGNATIONS OF FUNCTION] (21.0D)

Designations of function can be included in ADDED ENTRIES, e.g.:

- comp. compiler
- ed. editor
- ill. illustrator
- tr. translator

WITHDRAWALS

(a) When withdrawing a book or other library material use the ADDED ENTRIES (tracings) to find all the entries to be withdrawn from the CATALOGUES.

   Withdrawing catalogue cross references: If the entry you are withdrawing from the CATALOGUE is the only, i.e. last, one with that heading, you must check in the AUTHORITY FILES in order to withdraw any relevant cross references. Otherwise you will be directing library users to headings which do not exist in the catalogue.

   An automated cataloguing system can do these tasks for you.

(b) Make an entry in the withdrawals file, clearly marking the record 'withdrawn'. It is useful to keep a record of recent withdrawals in case queries arise later on. This is particularly true in the case where you are withdrawing records for an item which is believed to be missing, since it may reappear.

(c) If you are withdrawing part of a multi-copy or multi-volume work, alter the number of copies (volumes) held in the library as indicated in the CATALOGUE.

(d) Discharge the book from the circulation system and delete any records held by the circulation system.

(e) Obliterate all ownership markings from the item or stamp it WITHDRAWN.

(f) Be sure to remove any security devices.

BIBLIOGRAPHY

1 Library of Congress. *Name authorities cumulative microform edition*. Quarterly.
   — *CD-MARC names*. Service on CD-ROM. Quarterly. Announced 1989.

2 Gorman, Michael and Winkler, Paul W. (eds.). *Anglo-American cataloguing rules*. 2nd edition, 1988 revision. Chicago, ALA; Ottawa, CLA; London, LA, 1988. Paperback, hardback or ring-binder for future revisions.

3 British Library, Bibliographic Services Division. *Books in English*, 1971. Microfiche. Bimonthly and annual cumulations. From: BLBSD, 2 Sheraton Street, London W1V 4BH.

4 Library of Congress. *Library of Congress filing rules*, 1980.

5 Library Corporation. *Marcfiche*. Microfiche. Weekly index and updates with quarterly cumulative index.
   — *Bibliofile*. CD-ROM. Quarterly cumulations. Library Corporation, PO Box 40035, Washington DC 20016, USA.

6 Library of Congress. *National Union Catalog*. Available in various editions and formats. 1983 — microfiche. CD-ROM as *CDMARC Bibliographic*. 1989.

7 Library of Congress. *Shelflisting* 1987. Guidelines for allocating LC class numbers.

8 Library of Congress. *Geographic cutters*. 2nd edition, 1988. Microfiche. For allocating cutters to US place names and index to class G.

9 Library of Congress. *Cataloging service bulletin*. Quarterly. Most up-to-date information on LC cataloguing policy and publications.

10 Moys, E. M. *Moys classification scheme for law books*. 2nd edition. London, Butterworth, 1982.

11 Library of Congress. *LC classification schedules*. Separate schedules for main classes in various editions.

12 Library of Congress. *LC classification outline*. 5th edition, 1986. Key to LC classification; can aid in deciding which schedules to buy for a specialized library and in making guides for library users.

13 Library of Congress. *LC classification — additions and changes*. Quarterly — not cumulative. Shows developments in current LC classification policy. Cumulations are published by: Gale

Research Inc., Book Tower, Detroit, Michigan 48277 0748, USA. Paperback or microfiche. Gale also combine additions and changes into schedules, called 'super cumulations'. Expensive but save cataloguer's time. Paperback or microfiche.

14 British Library. *Name authority list.* Microfiche, monthly cumulations.

15 EBSCO. *The serials directory.* Annual. Printed or CD-ROM, includes class numbers for 113,000+ serial titles.

16 Library of Congress. *Library of Congress subject headings.* Annual currently in 3 vols. known as 'the big red books'. Weekly lists of new headings issued monthly – cumulated by Gale. Microform available with quarterly cumulations. — *CDMarc Subjects.* Quarterly. 1989: CD-ROM version which allows keyword searching; has MARC tags.

17 Library of Congress. *Subject cataloging manual. Subject headings.* 3rd edition, 1988. 2 vols., index and annual updates. Guidelines for allocating LCSH, written for LC's own staff but still important for complete understanding of LCSH.

Note. For further information on all LC's publications, two free annual catalogues are available from: Cataloging Distribution Service, Library of Congress, Washington D.C. 20541, USA. Access: catalogs and technical publications. MARC distribution services.

FURTHER USEFUL REFERENCES FOR CATALOGUING WITH AACR2 AND LC

18 Caster, Lillie D. *The classifier's guide to LC class H.* Subdivision techniques for the social sciences. Neal-Schuman, 1986.

19 Gorman, Michael. *The concise AACR2, 1988 revision.* Chicago, ALA, 1989.

20 Hunter, Eric J. *Examples illustrating AACR2.* 1988 revision. 2nd edition, London, LA, 1989.

21 Leong, Carol L.H. *Serials cataloguing handbook.* An illustrative guide to the use of AACR2 and LC rule interpretations. Chicago, ALA, 1989.

22 Maxwell, Margaret *Handbook for AACR2 1988 revision: explaining and illustrating the Anglo-American Cataloguing Rules.* Chicago, ALA, 1989.

INDEX

Page numbers followed by an asterisk (*) indicate major treatment of the topic. For the cataloguing/classification of a particular form/topic, look under the form/topic.

BNB *see* British National Bibliography
book numbers *see* cutter numbers; dates as part of LC class
   numbers
Books in English 8–9,* 13, 36, 45, 46
British Library 8, 43
British National Bibliography 8, 13

Call numbers *see* Library of Congress, class numbers
capitalization 54*
cards *see* Library of Congress cards
cartographic materials *see* maps
catalogue 10
catalogue entries 11,* 23–5, 53–4
catalogue input form 12,* 50
catalogue filing rules *see* filing
cataloguing in publication 8, 13,* 36, 39, 40, 45, 46
centralized cataloguing 14,* 23–5, 33, 39–41
change of name 4–5, 42–3
Christian names *see* forenames
CIP *see* cataloguing in publication
circulation numbers 12, 24, 50, 52, 76
class numbers *see* Library of Congress, class numbers
classification numbers *see* Library of Congress, class numbers
classified catalogue *see* shelflist
classmarks *see* Library of Congress, class numbers
collaborative works *see* joint authors
collections *see* edited works
collective titles *see* uniform titles
colloquia *see* conferences
COMARC 8, 39
compound names 4–5,* 28–9, 42–3
conferences 3, 15–16,* 17, 18, 25, 34, 42, 55, 74
congresses *see* conferences
contents notes 17
continuations 17*
conventions *see* conferences
copies, number of *see* number of copies
copy cataloguing *see* editing
copy number 1, 57
corporate bodies 3, 4–7, 15, 18,* 23, 28, 42–3

17.00

DATE DUE

HIGHSMITH 45-220